Milk to Mozzarella

written by
Mamie Goodson

photography by
Jimena Peck

A gallon of milk can turn into a ball of fresh, creamy mozzarella cheese in no time at all. The process is easy and fun.

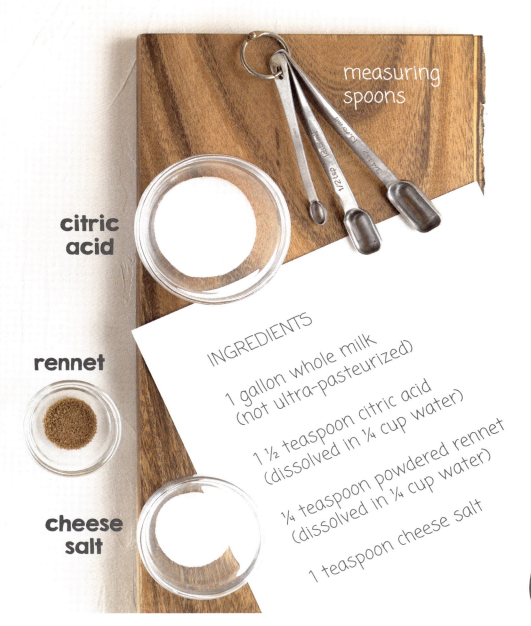

measuring spoons

citric acid

rennet

cheese salt

INGREDIENTS

1 gallon whole milk (not ultra-pasteurized)

1 ½ teaspoon citric acid (dissolved in ¼ cup water)

¼ teaspoon powdered rennet (dissolved in ¼ cup water)

1 teaspoon cheese salt

Milk is mostly made up of water, but it also contains solids like fat and protein. To make mozzarella—or any cheese—you must separate most of the solids from the water.

- ✓ **water**
- ✓ **fat**
- ✓ **protein**
- ✓ **sugar**
- ✓ **vitamins and minerals**

To launch the process, pour the milk into a big pot. The fresher the milk, the better the cheese will taste.

Next, mix citric acid with water and stir it into the milk. Citric acid sours the milk and helps prepare it for the next steps.

Then, begin to heat the milk on the stove. Stir it with a long spoon. Check the milk with a thermometer. When the milk reaches about 90 degrees, remove it from the heat.

The next step is to add something called rennet. Its job is to separate the milk into its liquid and solid parts.

Mix the rennet with water and stir it into the milk. Then, put a lid on the pot and wait.

Inside the pot, the rennet acts like a magnet. Its effect is automatic. The rennet draws the milk's fat and protein together into a mass of creamy white curd. The curd, which will become cheese, separates from the water and sugar in the milk. A thin, straw-colored liquid is left. It is called whey.

When the curd has set, cut it into small squares.

Next, cook the curds in the whey. With the spoon, move the curds around slowly. They float like fluffy white clouds. As the curds heat up, more whey is drawn out of them. When the whey reaches 105 degrees, remove the pot from the heat.

Scoop the curds into a bowl with a slotted spoon. Drain off as much whey as you can. Now, it's time to form your cheese!

Fresh mozzarella cheese is soft and stretchy. To make this texture, the curds must be heated and pressed.

Heat the curds in the microwave for 60 seconds. While they are still hot, an adult should press and fold them. Drain off any extra whey.

Heat the curds again, this time for 30 seconds. Press, fold, and drain them. Then, lift the curds and let them stretch down into the bowl.

Repeat this step until the cheese stretches and shines and no more whey is lost. Add salt to taste. Then, form the cheese into a ball of creamy mozzarella. Finally, drop the cheese ball into a bowl of very cold water to cool.

1

2

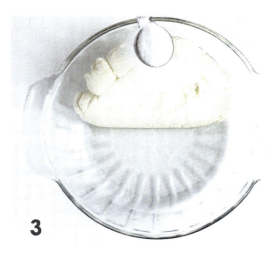
3

4

5

6

The last part of the cheese-making process may be the hardest. What will you do with your mozzarella ball? Cut off a hunk and eat it fresh? Or melt it onto a crispy pizza? You may just have to try both!

MORE

Cheeses range from hard to soft depending on how much water they contain. Hard cheeses have less liquid than soft cheeses. Several actions during the cheese-making process can lead to a lower moisture content. First, milk is separated into solid pieces called curd and a thin liquid called whey. Pressing the curd squeezes out more whey, which results in harder cheeses. Some cheeses are also washed in salt or soaked in saltwater. The salt pulls more moisture from the cheese. In addition, how long a cheese rests, or ages, affects its hardness.

Cheddar cheese goes through a unique hardening process. The name of the cheese comes from the verb *cheddaring*. Cheddaring involves cutting the curd into pieces, shaping those pieces into slabs, and then removing the whey by stacking and unstacking the slabs many times. Cheddar can be left to age for just a few months or for several years. Each step in the process adds to the final flavor of the cheese.

Milk to Mozzarella

A gallon of milk can turn into a ball of fresh, creamy mozzarella cheese in no time at all.

How does milk turn into a ball of cheese?

GEODES

Fundations® Alignment
93% Decodable at Level 2, Unit 16
Focus Concept
Double Vowel Syllable
(au, aw /ȯ/)

ISBN 978-1-64054-858-9

9 781640 548589

level 2 | module 4 | set 3
book 2

WIT & WISDOM®

Wit & Wisdom® Alignment
Good Eating (02.04)
Great Minds®